FIVE-MINUTE
MINDFULNESS
Walking

FIVE-MINUTE
MINDFULNESS

Walking

essays and exercises for mindfully
moving through the world

Douglas Baker

FAIR WINDS

Copyright © Quid Publishing 2016

First published in the United States of America in 2016 by
Fair Winds Press, a member of
Quarto Publishing Group USA Inc.
100 Cummings Center
Suite 406-L
Beverly, Massachusetts 01915-6101
Telephone: (978) 282-9590
Fax: (978) 283-2742
QuartoKnows.com

10 9 8 7 6 5 4 3 2 1

ISBN: 978-1-59233-746-0

Conceived, designed, and produced by
Quid Publishing
Part of The Quarto Group
Level 1 Ovest House
58 West Street
Brighton BN1 2RA
England

Design and layout by Lindsey Johns
Illustrations by Tilly and Tonwen Jones

Printed in China

To Yoganand,
Shobhan, Danna,
and Lucie, and all the other
teachers, seekers, and fellow
travelers who've encouraged
me, and so many others,
on the path.

Contents

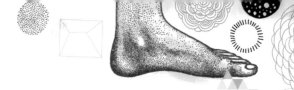

Introduction

WHAT IS MINDFULNESS?

Mindfulness is a state of mind. It's about noticing your thoughts and actions in a non-judgmental, open way, as they happen, so that you don't get lost in distractions, reactions, or worries. In mindfulness, you use the mind's natural capacity to be attentive, non-reactive, and relaxed. You then connect to what's actually important, inside and around you. It's an intelligence we all have but often don't use.

Mindfulness is typically accessed through meditation. From this open, focused mind state, we more clearly distinguish right actions from fruitless struggle. We get clearer about when we're trying to control things we can't possibly control, and better at perceiving our inner reactions before they become regrettable outward actions. We begin to see how much of our stress is created inside the mind. And we start to experience a stillness of mind and body that doesn't

> MINDFULNESS IS A WAY OF USING THE MIND SO THE MIND DOESN'T USE YOU.

require the glass of wine, medication, or hour of massage. With a little persistence and patience, a kind of balance and nobility is glimpsed in the mind.

Mindfulness is sometimes falsely equated with being passive and disconnected. Not so. It's not about becoming checked-out, dreamily floating on a cloud. Mindfulness is a way of being present, focused, and skillful with what's happening in your life, with less struggle. It's an empowering tool for people living active, engaged lives. It helps us to act more efficiently, waste less energy in mind-made dramas, and orient to what's real. "The truth will support us," a teacher of mine once said. "A fantasy will not." Mindfulness helps us find what's true.

And perhaps best of all, it's free, organic, and locally produced. It's right under your nose, or in the sole of your foot. It's always there to tap into, no matter where you find yourself. It's not a magic cure, but it is a simple, cumulative method of orienting differently toward life and life's challenges.

How Mindfulness Works

Mindfulness happens in switching the mind from busy "thinking and planning" mode to simple "observing" mode. You can start by directing your attention to a neutral object or process, like your breathing, or the movement of your feet. You then do your best to observe the flow of sensations as you breathe or walk—*which is different from thinking about it.* You simply notice. Then, before you know it, you'll probably find you're thinking again. No problem. Just turn back to observing the breath or the feet. You do this again and again, in a relaxed, unhurried, non-perfectionistic way—simply returning to observing.

Why the emphasis on this odd state of non-thinking? The thinking mode can dominate our waking hours in unhelpful ways. We get caught up in pointless thoughts about the past, worries about the future, imaginary conversations in which we brilliantly tell the boss *how it really is*—all distracting us from being present for what's happening in any moment.

Thoughts drive our moods and emotions, and anxious thoughts produce anxious body states—increasing muscle tension, heart rate, and blood pressure. Through mindfulness, we observe our thoughts and gain a clearer awareness of our thought patterns, which can unhook us from detrimental habits. Mindfulness helps us simply to feel what life brings our way, take a breath, and then decide on a course of action. This is a major step toward mental and emotional well-being.

BENEFITS OF MINDFULNESS

According to the American Psychiatric Association, research has reliably established links between mindfulness practice and the following benefits:

- Lower rates of anxiety and depression

- Boosts in working memory and improved focus and attention

- Reduced emotional volatility

- Increased cognitive flexibility and information-processing speed

- Enhanced self-insight, morality, intuition, and fear modulation

- Increased immune functioning

- Increased empathy and compassion and improved relationship satisfaction

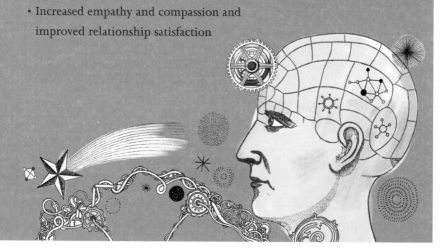

The Practice of Mindful Walking

Mindfulness is commonly achieved through meditation, a practice that dates back at least a few thousand years, to early Buddhists in what is now India. (Other cultures around the globe have practiced similar mind-focusing methods to achieve higher states of consciousness for millennia.) Meditation is classically done in a seated position, eyes closed, with attention focused on the breath. But there is also a long tradition of taking the practice on the road— mindful walking, the focus of this book.

> "BETWEEN STIMULUS
> AND RESPONSE, THERE IS A
> SPACE. IN THAT SPACE IS OUR
> POWER TO CHOOSE OUR RESPONSE.
> IN OUR RESPONSE LIES OUR
> GROWTH AND FREEDOM."
>
> —VIKTOR FRANKL

For some, mindful walking has certain advantages. Many people struggle to focus in seated meditation. Because so little is happening, the mind is all too ready to wander off—back to thinking. Let's face it, observing your breath is only so interesting.

Mindful walking provides more for the mind to connect to. There's something far more concrete to focus on: movements of the body. Thus it tends to be more user-friendly for the novice. Another advantage is that mindful walking doesn't require special time set aside. Many of us want to meditate but find it surprisingly hard to "find" time for it on a consistent basis. I've heard many then sadly conclude, "I can't meditate." Walking with mindfulness frees the would-be meditator to roam far and wide, cultivating mindfulness in the process of walking itself.

So if the idea of seated meditating is about as appealing as paying taxes or visiting the dentist, things are looking up. You're officially off the hook. Lace up your walking shoes, and prepare to meditate. You'll be a mobile Zen ninja in no time.

About This Book

The current pace of life sees us struggling to manage demands for our attention, often leaving us frazzled and overwhelmed. This book is designed to introduce the practice of mindful walking, and mindfulness, to gain greater perspective, clarity, and balance in mind and body. And to suit even the busiest schedule, each short essay and exercise is meant to be read and digested, or completed, in about five minutes. Don't try too hard to be mindful or to control the experience. Just read, walk, observe, and let go of looking for the "right" result.

"IF YOU LET GO A LITTLE,
YOU WILL HAVE A LITTLE PEACE.

IF YOU LET GO A LOT, YOU WILL
HAVE A LOT OF PEACE.

IF YOU LET GO COMPLETELY, YOU
WILL HAVE COMPLETE PEACE."

—AJAHN CHAH

① WALKING AS MEDITATION

Mindfulness is often symbolized by a Buddha statue: someone seated, in deep concentration. The image is a wonderful reminder of mindfulness. But we could say there's also a curse of the Buddha statue: it implies that real meditation happens only when seated. Mindfulness, however, is a state of mind. It's not about a particular position. Walking meditation cultivates mindfulness in the flow of movement and sensation. We just notice what happens, without judging, planning, or any other thinking. We zero in to carefully observe the sensations that naturally happen in stepping. No special walking technique—we just step.

What's special is the mind: a focused, relaxed awareness, receiving the experience in moment-to-moment bits, like watching the frames of a video in slow motion. We become extraordinarily clear and attentive. Busy mind fades into the background. In each step, closely observed, mindfulness is happening. It's that simple.

Mindfulness in Walking

Most of the time we are lost in thought, in a mental world of opinions, memories, dreams, and schemes. There's nothing necessarily wrong with being carried away by the stream of thoughts. Walking along the beach in summer, we can enjoy a reverie about last year's trip, or what we'd like for dinner. Meditators allow themselves plenty of guilt-free daydreaming. The mindfulness authorities don't come and write a citation. But if our only mode of mind is thinking, we may not be entirely present in our actual life. We're in a kind of virtual reality. It *relates* to real life, but it's one step removed: it exists in the mind. Thoughts about life are not life; thoughts about your cat are not your cat. Our feet are on the ground, but we're not mentally grounded.

Mindfulness is a way to stabilize the mind in what's real. And mindful walking allows us to create the stability of mindfulness in virtually any setting. We use sensations, sounds, and sights to ground the mind. Once grounded, we can notice beauty, attune to those we care about, and make skillful decisions.

USE THE BODY TO ANCHOR THE MIND TO THE PRESENT MOMENT— TO WHAT'S REAL AND WHAT'S IMPORTANT.

Through using walking as meditation, we begin to connect our mental world with our physical. The mind and body affect each other in so many ways, and the practice of mindful walking invites them into a working relationship. Mind, meet body. Body, say hello to mind. Oftentimes, they're barely acquainted, even though they're living under the same roof.

Once introduced, they can begin to collaborate. Mindful walking uses the body to better know and understand the mind, and the mind to better know and understand the body. We can then create what's called mindfulness in the body—the best of both worlds. Through our practice we begin to sense an order, intelligence, and mind–body cohesion inside. With each mindful step we reinforce this harmony.

FOCUSING ON CONTACT
WITH THE GROUND

Find a place to stand where you can close your eyes for a minute or two. (If necessary, leave your eyes open but defocus them, looking at a space on the floor about ten feet in front of you.)

- Investigate: where are sensations strongest in your body? Probably the bottom of the feet. Take 30 seconds to notice, in good detail, what you feel there. Tingling? Pressure? Warmth? Simply take in your impressions. Mindfulness has begun.

- Now, we'll start with a single step. Slowly, ridiculously slowly, begin to lift one foot—as if it's glued to the floor and you must gradually peel it off—and notice the sensations.

- Notice rolling onto the ball of the foot, the feeling of lifting. Do it slowly. Remember the astronaut first stepping off the ladder onto the moon? Like that.

- Observe the feeling of your foot moving through space, and then—contact! Check out those sensations as your foot comes back to terra firma.

- Congratulate yourself profusely. You've taken your first mindful walk.

The Mindfulness Paradox

As you practiced, you may have noticed a little unauthorized thinking. Don't curse yourself as incapable of even minding one step. "Wandering mind" is the pattern you've cultivated your entire life. Why would we expect the mind not to wander now?

Mindfulness happens when we focus on sensations, but also when we notice the attention wandering and the mind thinking. It's all equally good mindfulness. Whatever you notice—foot, movement, or brazen thinking—mindfulness is there. We see that there's a paradox in mindfulness: we intend just to notice, and we accept that thinking happens. Find a way to love that paradox, or you will suffer. Our goal is not to stamp out thinking. When you notice thinking, just smile.

Simple Movements Simplify the Mind

The human thought process has been compared to a waterfall—an endless flow of thoughts. Often we're carried off in those waters without a paddle. You start off thinking about what to make for dinner and you end up reliving a trip to the Grand Canyon. You wonder, "How on Earth did I get here?" This happens through the associative nature of the mind. Our minds are great at associating one thing with another. This is what allows children to learn that ice is cold. The child associates one thing, ice, with the sensation of feeling cold. It is the foundation of learning, and it is very helpful.

> "I HAVE BEEN THROUGH SOME TERRIBLE THINGS IN MY LIFE, SOME OF WHICH ACTUALLY HAPPENED."
>
> **—MARK TWAIN**

Except associations can sweep us away, so that we find we can't stop thinking or worrying about something, or we needlessly imagine future disasters. We're dragged behind the randomly associating mind, in the words of the poet Hafiz, "like a broken man behind a farting camel."

Being mindful of simple movements helps us to climb out of the cascading thoughts. It simplifies the mind, one action at a time. When overstimulated, we guide our attention purely to simple movement—picking up a teacup, or taking a few steps. Out of the random associations pinging around the mind, we drop into a state of simplicity.

My foot is stepping. That's all I'm aware of. And then notice: Did the mind get quieter? Just for a moment? The busy mind is like the surface of a lake on a stormy day, waves churning restlessly. When we bring attention down, into the simple movements of the body, it is like diving beneath the stormy surface of the water. There's still movement at that depth—but it's slower, simpler. If we pay attention, we experience the mind growing quiet.

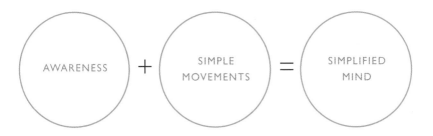

AWARENESS + SIMPLE MOVEMENTS = SIMPLIFIED MIND

TAKE FIVE

TRYING DIFFERENT
WALKING SPEEDS

Find a place to start where you have a clear path ahead for 30 to 60 feet.

• Stand with your feet about hip-width apart, and slightly unlock the knees, noticing the leg muscles gripping to keep the legs upright.

• Staying attentive, begin to walk forward at your normal pace, noticing what you feel in the body. Walk to the end of your path and back. Pause for a brief assessment: how much sensation were you able to perceive at that speed? It may have been a bit of a blur.

• Now walk the same path again, quite a bit slower—roughly half your normal rate. Observe the sensations at this speed. Can you better perceive the components of walking—landing, shifting, lifting?

• Now, begin to walk at a speed so slow—think molasses crawling out of a jar—that you can stay tuned to the details of soles of feet, leg muscles, and knees. When you're done, assess which rate of speed helps you stay most focused. This is a good start for getting to know how mindfulness works for you in walking.

SOMETIMES
WE MOVE TOO
FAST TO NOTICE
WHAT'S ACTUALLY
HAPPENING IN
OUR LIFE.

TAKE FIVE

LABELING SENSATIONS WITH ONE WORD

This simple practice is a great way to connect the mind and body.

Begin by standing still, with your eyes closed if it is practical to do so. Bring your attention to the feelings of the body. In your mind, silently label the sensations you notice. Boil it down to one word per sensation. Don't obsess over the "right" word—many sensations are complex, but for simplicity of mind, choose just one. Where you feel socks around feet, the word could be "contact." Where you feel your sweater around your shoulders, the word might be "warmth," or "soft."

Gradually lean into a first step and begin to walk, stepping slowly. Label each sensation and now label actions too. As perception sharpens, we see there are a lot of actions in the simplest walk. A foot is "lifting," "moving," then "contacting." A knee is "bending," "gripping," and "stretching."

Allow your awareness to wander through the body, noticing the action of the arms swinging; the air on the skin; the facial muscles forming an expression. There's far more going on in any one moment than we generally notice—because we're often not actually with the body when we walk. We're somewhere else, at least in the mind.

> "HE LIVED AT A LITTLE DISTANCE FROM HIS BODY."
>
> —JAMES JOYCE, DUBLINERS, 1914

Walking as Meditation

2 WALKING TO SETTLE THE MIND

Mindful walking takes a most ordinary activity, and uses it to cultivate a state of mind that's extraordinarily beneficial. As we meditate on walking, there's a dissolving of unhelpful habits of the mind; worrying, judging, regretting, and drifting into unhelpful fantasies all begin to fall away. That's the first benefit. Then mindfulness nurtures a gradual, steady transformation. Something new arises: beneficial mind habits.

You begin to cultivate concentration, focus, and clarity. You grow an ability to notice without jumping to conclusions or judgments. Undistracted attention becomes more available. You experience more control of the mind. You gradually turn the mind into a reliable, steady ally, from the easily distracted, drunken-sailor mind many of us struggle with.

Mindful walking is training for the mind. The mind begins to follow the intelligence and logic of the body's movement patterns. The mind's patterns take on the qualities of walking: steady, controlled, linear, and balanced.

The Body Has No Opinion

In mindful walking we feel the body without forming an opinion on it. We simply experience the body as it is. We refrain from adding opinions, like "I look weird" or "I'm strong." This is the practice of nonjudgment: noticing, without a liking or not-liking position. You can like things on Facebook, but that's not our intention here.

It's not that opinions are evil. Sometimes, we need opinions. Is it safe to cross the street right now? We need an opinion. Has this fish been in the fridge too long? Opinion, please. Our goal is balance: to have opinions when they're helpful, and to be free of opinions when they're not helpful—when they're just added mind-chatter. This is in recognition that our opinions often create mental suffering. If we look in the mirror and

"ALL WE WANT ARE THE FACTS, MA'AM."

—JOE FRIDAY, DRAGNET

think to ourselves, "I look so old," we're judging ourselves on something we can't do anything about: the aging process. Not helpful. *Causes suffering.*

With mindful walking, we scrub the mind, temporarily, of opinions. Our intention is to nurture "pure awareness" of the body in motion. We can then apply this no-opinion approach in life situations where an opinion doesn't help. Of course, it's the nature of the mind to think—it secretes thoughts the way the heart pumps blood. We can't stop it thinking. For this reason, we use thoughts simply to label our experience, without judging. As we step, and notice pressure on the foot, we think, "pressure." As we lift the foot to take a step, we simply think, "lifting." Not "good lifting," or "I love this lifting." Just "lifting."

Letting Mindfulness Come and Go as You Step

Mindfulness is a not a permanent state. In fact, it's not even really a thing. It's a process of paying attention. We don't have to stress about losing it, like a wallet. It's more accurate to say that we go into it and go out of it. When we go out, we know we'll be back. The last thing you want to do is obsess about your mindfulness practice, holding on with a death-grip. We just relax, walk, and notice what's happening.

Like a good parent, be somewhat permissive with your mind, but not neglectful. As you walk, allow your awareness to behave like the adolescent it is, constantly changing its mind about what's cool. Don't fight its tendency to be unpredictable and continuously shifting focus. For example, one moment you'll walk and make a good effort to focus on stepping or on the colors of a garden you're passing. The mind zeroes in, absorbed and concentrated. You're Mr. or Ms. Zen Mind. You can't believe how focused you are, not a thought in sight. Then suddenly you realize you're thinking about

EASY COME

EASY GO

EASY COME
BACK

how mindful you are. You've lost it, just when you thought you were enlightened! But, the moment you notice you're thinking and planning, you're mindful again. You remember that you're walking, and each step settles the mind. Easy come, easy go—and easy come back.

Adopt a non-discriminatory mindfulness policy. Whether you're observing walking movements, sensations, sounds, colors, or your own self-impressed thoughts, mindfulness is there. Sure, mindfulness without thoughts is, in theory, more "pure." But that's mindfulness on an Olympic level. For most people, the practice is perfectly imperfect. It's kind of a revolving door, and you notice going in and out of mindfulness. You keep the door unlocked. When you step out, it's like you've hung your sign on the door: "Back in a few minutes."

TAKING THE PUPPY (MIND) FOR A WALK

Let's take the puppy for a walk. Imagine that you are a puppy trainer and your wandering mind is a puppy. The practice is to walk with this puppy, allowing it some leash to wander (think), and then to patiently lead it back—placing your attention back on walking.

Find a place to walk where your path is clear and you won't be in anyone's way. This could be anywhere—at a transit station while you wait for a bus or train, in a park, or in your home.

Pause and gather your contingent:

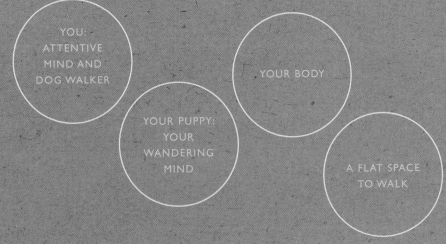

YOU: ATTENTIVE MIND AND DOG WALKER

YOUR PUPPY: YOUR WANDERING MIND

YOUR BODY

A FLAT SPACE TO WALK

Set out your intention: to focus on the body, its movements, and contact with the surface you're walking on. Add the intention to notice when your puppy-mind tries to run free.

Begin to step slowly, focusing on movements and contact with the surface of the floor. Focus on these details as you move. This is mindfulness in the body.

Stay attentive for the golden moment, when you've noticed that the puppy has bolted: you're thinking about something else.

This is golden because it's very helpful; mindfulness has perceived the thinking mind running away. The mind is observing itself—a high, and highly valuable, state of consciousness. Don't judge it as a failure. See the victory. It's another paradox of mindfulness: we take the "failure" to stay focused and make it a success. We've successfully noticed what the mind is doing—wandering.

No dog trainer can prevent a puppy from bolting. They can only train it to come back, by reeling in the leash. No one can fully prevent the mind from wandering—we can only notice and bring it back, patiently.

Walk, notice, reel in the puppy-mind. Give yourself a friendly pat. Good dog.

Your Brain on Mindfulness

Mindfulness has many observable benefits for the brain—the organ that is home to the mind. MRI scans allow researchers to monitor brain activity, and track the brain's responses to mindfulness.

Research has shown that mindfulness:

HELPS TRAIN THE BRAIN TO BE HAPPIER

Certain parts of the brain are active during times of negative and positive moods: the left side of the prefrontal cortex (PFC) is associated with optimistic and energized moods; the right side is more active when we're depressed and anxious. A 2003 study at the University of Massachusetts Medical School, which investigated the effects of mindfulness practice on these regions, showed a significant increase in left-side PFC activity in participants who had taken an eight-week meditation program, when assessed four months later.

INCREASES RESILIENCE

Practicing mindfulness has been shown to condition the brain for resilience—the ability to respond well to change, challenges, and stress, and return to steady baseline functioning quickly. In 2015, a team led by neuroscientist Yi-Yuan Tang found that a group given just two and a half hours' mindful meditation practice showed increased activity in the part of the prefrontal cortex associated with self-regulation and learning from past experiences. They were also less distractible, compared to a group given relaxation training.

CHANGES THE BRAIN'S STRESS CENTER

Mindfulness practice is associated with helpful changes in the part of the brain that plays a key role in depression, anxiety, and aggression—the amygdala. A healthy amygdala increases the brain's ability to respond to difficulties with less reactivity. A 2015 study at the University of Pittsburgh's Center for Neuroscience showed a connection between mindful meditation training and healthier, less reactive amygdala responses.

CAN CHANGE BRAIN STRUCTURES IN EIGHT WEEKS

A group of Harvard neuroscientists found in 2011 that just eight weeks of meditation practice can positively affect physical structures in your brain. They recorded startling changes in the regions of participants' brains involved in learning, memory, emotion regulation, sense of self, empathy, and stress.

Wise Walking, Easy on Ourselves

The human mind has the capacity to create many things. Unfortunately, one of them is stress. One way we do this is through a pattern of thinking using the "comparing mind," when we relentlessly evaluate ourselves against others. We often don't even realize we're doing it. It's a repetitive narrative we could title: *Further Reflections on How I Measure Up, and Mostly Don't, by Me.*

As you walk down the street, you pass someone who you judge as "having it together." *Look at that fellow, I'll bet his career is really on fire. Me, I just haven't made much of myself.* A moment ago you felt fine. Now, nothing about you has changed, except the comparing mind has kicked in, altering self-perception. Unpleasant emotion comes with the thoughts, which further convinces you the judgments are valid. We think it and feel it, so it must be true.

To reduce self-judgment, make it a regular practice to notice what you're thinking about as you walk. If you perceive thoughts comparing yourself to other people, ask yourself: Are these thoughts helpful? Are they adding something constructive?

TAKE FIVE · HELPFUL COMPARING

When gripped by unhelpful comparing, use mindful walking to disrupt the thought pattern.

Bring attention to the details and sensations of walking and the mind will shift. Now you're just noticing. Each step is not better or worse than any other, it's just a step—this step.

As you continue to notice your movements with mindfulness, you may begin to feel better, a little lighter mentally and emotionally. The mental spotlight of self-scrutiny has been turned down a few thousand kilowatts.

As you continue on a walk, compare how you feel walking mindfully to how it felt in the comparing mind. That's a helpful comparison. In mindfulness it's called noticing cause and effect, or how things work. It's also called cultivating wisdom.

3 WALKING IS SENSATIONAL

Throughout history, philosophers, writers, and thinkers have sought a reliable path to inner peace. The great teachers of mindful walking say it's possible in one simple step. When I'm leading a mindfulness retreat and mention this one step to inner peace, the participants lean forward in anticipation: "What is it?" they want to know. "Can it really happen in just one step? What is this incredible, transformational step?"

Answer: This step. The step you're stepping. I then enjoy the looks of confusion: is this some annoying Zen riddle?

From the conventional view it seems inner peace has to be more complicated. But as we focus on sensations of a step, the focusing itself quiets the mind. Peace happens. Sensational peace, as it were. We can't let the mind overthink it and tell us it can't be that simple. If we do, we've lost the focus, and with it, the peace.

Know That You Are Walking

Anytime we walk, we can calm the mind by guiding attention to the physical sensations of walking. Things immediately get simpler. The mind anchors to what's real, not random thoughts. The beauty of walking meditation is it happens in the flow of other activities. It's an active, health-promoting way to cultivate mindfulness. As we walk to the gym or run on the treadmill we bring our observing mind to the movements of our legs. Walking into the grocery store we notice what we can hear and smell. Going from the office to the car or up the stairs to tuck the kids into bed we can create a mini-practice of 30 seconds. We don't need to "find" any more time. We use little bits of the time we have differently.

Those bits, added together, become a big change: a little more balance between the very busy and the spacious. When we need it most, when we're feeling most stretched, we draw attention to the sensations of the breath, the feelings in the body, to our feet moving, and in that spacious mind, achieved through simply noticing, there's the possibility of a little rejuvenation.

"WHEN WE WALK, WE KNOW WE ARE WALKING."

—THE BUDDHA, QUOTED BY THICH NHAT HANH

Many people tell me they can't find time to practice mindfulness, because they have so much to do. "There's so much going on," I hear people saying again and again (myself included). Going to the gym, to work, grocery shopping, parenting, staying on top of incoming emails. We all experience how busy and even overwhelming modern life has become. You've probably had, or overheard, one of these conversations:

> *How's life?*
> Busy.
> *How's work?*
> Crazy. Just nuts.

Many of us recognize the need to find an island of quiet in a packed schedule. But when I speak with someone who is interested in mindfulness, the sticking point is often: "But when?" Sometimes I see fear in their eyes as they anticipate that I'm about to pressure them to jam one more activity into their day—to hurry up and meditate!

TAKE FIVE

MINDFULNESS IN THE
FLOW OF SENSATIONS

Any time you're out for a walk, you can easily drop into mindful walking.
All you need to do is turn your attention to the flow of sensations. As
you walk, begin by noticing which sensation is most vivid.

IS IT THE SUN
ON YOUR FACE
CREATING A
PENETRATING
HEAT?

ARE YOUR SORE
FEET SPEAKING
THE LOUDEST TO
YOU, ASKING FOR
A REST?

IS THE HEAVY
PRESSURE OF THE
SHOULDER BAG
YOU'RE CARRYING
THE STRONGEST
SENSATION?

In each moment as we walk, we keep checking: What's most vivid,
now? And now?

Notice the sensations as a chorus of voices, one chiming in first, then
another, or perhaps all together at once. Remember, you don't need to
plan or control what you're mindful of. This should be relaxing. Just
allow your attention to drift from one sensation to the next and back
again. You follow the song the sensations are singing.

There's a stress-reducing effect in this practice, as you step out of your thoughts that create stress, and slide the mind into a more neutral, less agitated state. Just for a few minutes, let go of trying to figure out what to do with this or that problem. Notice if your feeling of stress seems to ease as you allow the time to just be with sensation.

Relax any unnecessary tension in the body. Let your shoulders settle, your face relax, your hands open and soften.

Next, shift attention to noticing which sensations are the most subtle.

IS IT THE FEELING OF THE HAIR ON YOUR HEAD?

OR THE CLOTHING ON YOUR SKIN?

IS IT THE BREATH ENTERING AND LEAVING YOUR NOSTRILS?

OR PERHAPS THE FEELING OF EYELASHES ON YOUR EYELIDS?

After each sensational walk, check in with yourself and see if you feel more spacious, more at ease, lighter. You've taken the walking cure, and it will encourage you to do it again the next time you're walking.

USING THE FIVE SENSES

One of my favorite practices in mindful walking is called touring the senses. We use the five senses themselves as the object of concentration. This creates a wonderfully focused effect in the mind, as we explore a kaleidoscope of sound, smell, taste, sight, and, of course, touch sensations.

Touring the senses uses the barrage of sensory input, which can often be quite distracting, as an aid to presence, focus, and steadiness of mind. We can do this in mindful walking, as long as we don't have to be too careful of where we're stepping. So, for this practice, choose a place to walk that's relatively smooth and free of obstacles.

Before you begin walking, imagine your observing self is seated on a steady platform inside the mind. It's sitting and watching intently, like in a movie theater, ready for the show to begin.

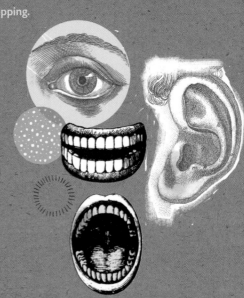

SOUND

SMELL

TASTE

SIGHT

TOUCH

- Begin to walk slowly. As you step, notice the different moving parts: sounds, smells, sights, taste, and touch sensations. These sensory parts are changing, coming and going, but the observing self is steady.

- Next, isolate your attention on one sense at a time. Start with sounds. As you walk, listen intently to each sound that arrives at your ears. Experience each as pure sound, without focusing on where it came from. A car-horn sound arrives. Notice its qualities (sharp, shrill, loud) without

thoughts about a "car horn," because that is a thought about the sound. Your goal is pure sound.

- Do the same with the next series of sounds, taking in each as cleanly as possible. After a few moments, pause and notice how the listening practice has affected you. You may observe a sense of quiet and simplicity in the mind.

- Continue to walk, and take turns with the other senses. After each instance of "pure receiving," notice the effects.

Three Stages of Walking Meditation

We can think of meditation happening in three stages and to progress through these, we must make use of our senses. In "concentration," the first stage, we focus on one sensation at a time, to improve control of the mind. In the second, "open attention"—or mindfulness—we notice whatever comes into our awareness, without picking a focus point. These stages create clarity of perception and lead to the third—"insight," a heightened awareness of cause and effect around us. It's useful to know the three stages as you practice.

1) CONCENTRATION

- **Essence:** Basic control of the mind

- **Quality:** Focused and narrow, like the beam of a flashlight

- **Technique:** Close attention to one experience; eyes may be focused

- **Benefits:** Improves attention; reduces distractibility

2) OPEN ATTENTION (MINDFULNESS)

- **Essence:** A sweet feeling of not always needing to be in control

- **Quality:** Open, receptive, and all-inclusive, like a panoramic view

- **Technique:** Wide-open awareness of the five senses; eyes defocused

- **Benefits:** Relaxes the mind; cultivates flexibility and non-reactivity

3) INSIGHT

- **Essence:** Learning what life has to teach us

- **Quality:** Contemplative, wise, and rational; seeing cause and effect

- **Technique:** Pausing to reflect during or right after meditation to observe the effects of the practice; eyes closed

- **Benefits:** Helps us to see the results of actions more clearly; enables us to make more skillful choices

As you practice mindful walking, work with the three stages in sequence, because they build on each other. Once learned, you can be creative and playfully shift among them.

PRACTICING THE THREE STAGES

Start walking, and focus intently on one experience, such as sensations in the feet. After a minute or two, shift to the second stage, allowing your attention to go panoramic, unfocused. Walk and let your spacious awareness receive anything that happens—a sound, a smell, a sensation, a thought—not locking onto anything for more than a few seconds. Notice each one like a bird flying through your sky. Finally, stop, pause, and close your eyes. Take in the effects of the practice. Notice: Is the mind more quiet, or less? Are you more, or less, relaxed? Do you feel in any way better, or worse, than before you began?

4 POSITIVE MIND STATES

Mindful walking is an opportunity to bring out the best in the mind. Each time we walk, we not only wipe the mind clean of negative states, but plant the seed for positive states of mind that help us live a more balanced, focused, happy, and skillful life. Each step is a gentle nudge to remember that we have a choice: take our chances with what the mind brings us, or populate the mind with states that are helpful.

To make walking practice an incubator for positive mind states, we need to do two things. First, learn to identify beneficial and unbeneficial mind states, and make it a regular practice to notice them. Second, create a link in the mind between mindful walking and positive mind states. It might be as simple as reminding ourselves, each time we practice, "Mindfully walking, I cultivate helpful mind states." Each mindful walk then reinforces this link.

Beneficial and Unbeneficial Mind States

Mind states are common mental patterns that all human beings share. They're like the mind's skeleton—a background structure, largely invisible, but very important. They're the foundation upon which the mind rests. Understanding and working with them is crucial for mental and physical well-being. They consist of two simple categories. Here is a brief overview.

Beneficial: Patience, trust, confidence, humor, generosity, flexibility, curiosity, forgiveness, kindness, empathy, gratitude, diligence, focus, honesty, wonder, joy.

Unbeneficial: Impatience, fear, pessimism, greed, anger, resentment, jealousy, self-pity, judgmentalism, rigidity, self-centeredness.

These mind states are like the air we breathe—we generally don't even notice them. But we view the world, and ourselves, through them, so they have a powerful effect. Like the air, if they're polluted with negativity, there's a toxic effect on the mind and body. As we cultivate the positive mind states, we're more healthy, the world looks friendlier, and a happy life seems more possible.

LEVERAGING BENEFICIAL MIND STATES

To leverage beneficial mind states, try these practices:

- Notice and identify mind states as they arise; or ask yourself, "What mind state am I in now?"

- Observe how each mind state affects you on different levels. How does fear, for example, affect your body, your decisions, your effectiveness, and worldview?

- When you notice an unhelpful mind state, choose a helpful state, name it, and affirm your intention to grow it.

- Affirm a chosen mind state by silently naming it—as in, "I'm cultivating gratitude."

"I HAVE GREAT FAITH IN A SEED. CONVINCE ME THAT YOU HAVE A SEED THERE, AND I AM PREPARED TO EXPECT WONDERS."

—HENRY D. THOREAU

- Notice if your inner weather brightens even just slightly as you invite a beneficial mind state. We're not seeking a complete transformation. We're just planting a seed, so look for a tiny sprout of something positive.

- Choose a beneficial mind state to emphasize each time you practice mindful walking.

Positive Mind States

TAKE FIVE

A POSITIVE MIND STATE
IN EACH WALK

In this practice, we'll look deeper inside, beyond physical sensations, to glimpse mind states. Because mind states drive our attitudes, behavior, and many of our emotions, it's helpful to perceive them and, at times, shift them.

Let's begin. Locate your walk, start moving, and fire up your noticing mind. Bring close attention to the sensations of walking, changing as you step.

Now direct that careful attention to noticing your mind state. It's far less concrete than a sensation, so at first it may be difficult. It's a little like noticing what the inside of the mouth tastes like: at first we might say, "Nothing." But if we attend closely, we might notice a slight sour taste. Sometimes the mind is sour, but we don't notice.

Examine carefully what the condition of your mind seems to be. You might detect, for example, a slight impatience with this practice. Noticing it, you've tuned into a mind state. As you continue walking, keep checking your mind state. Your attention probably can't focus steadily on it, because you've got to watch where you're going. Let attention flow back and forth between physical matters, thoughts, and the mind state.

Thoughts provide clues about the mind state, because they are an expression of it. If you notice amused thoughts ("Mindful walking must look quite comical . . ."), no doubt a mind state of humor is there. See if you can connect to it.

Now, try mixing your own special sauce. How about sprinkling a little gratitude on the amused thoughts? You might work your way into a grateful mind state with a thought: "I'm grateful I'm willing to try something as eccentric as mindful walking." Notice if a sense of gratitude bubbles up. You'll have felt feelings of gratitude before, but you're beginning to perceive the mind state that underpins them.

In this way, you can begin to see more of the working parts of the mind, which create many attitudes and beliefs. As we are more aware of these mind states, we can cultivate those that empower us.

LOVING KINDNESS

Walking meditation is medicinal for the body and mind, and also the spirit. We can use the practice to cultivate love and happiness. This happens through making an offering to those we pass as we walk. It's a tradition in the meditative arts known as loving kindness, or *metta*—the practice of silently offering kindness or love to others. In order to "give" love, we first summon a loving feeling in ourselves, as we can't give what we don't have in the first place. Thus, we are steeping ourselves in the good vibrations we deliver to others. It's like working in a coffee shop and having the easiest possible access to coffee.

"ADMIT SOMETHING. EVERYONE YOU MEET, YOU SAY TO THEM, 'LOVE ME.' OF COURSE, YOU DO NOT SAY THIS OUT LOUD, OTHERWISE SOMEONE WOULD CALL THE COPS."

—HAFIZ

On your next walk, hold your torso upright—dignified and open. Invite a steady rhythm in your breath, and prepare for stealth spirituality. As you approach living beings—human, animal, or even those of the plant world—silently offer them good wishes of your choice. Give what you would most appreciate receiving. Don't look directly at them if they're people; just hold them in awareness as you pass. Here are some of my favorite offerings:

"MAY YOU BE
TRULY HAPPY."

"MAY YOU BE
SAFE AND
PROTECTED."

"MAY YOU GIVE
AND RECEIVE
LOVE."

"MAY YOU BE
HEALTHY AND
FREE."

"MAY YOU LET
YOUR FREAK
FLAG FLY."

"MAY YOU
ROCK
TO THE FULLEST
EXTENT PERMISSIBLE
UNDER LOCAL
ORDINANCES."

As always in walking meditation, it's important to notice the effect it has on you.

Although this practice may feel silly, remember that new things often feel unnatural at first. Observe the effects, including a before/after comparison of your inner weather. Is it a little brighter, more humorous, or more loving inside?

Practice a little more, offering good wishes to yourself. You deserve a cup too.

Lost in Thoughts, Found in Beauty

Sharing Moments

On a hiking trip in New Hampshire, I woke in my tent to a stunning fall day, cool and crisp. I was camped by a mountain brook in a remote part of the National Forest. I had good food, dark chocolate, green tea, and just enough gear—positioned for pleasures in a gorgeous place.

After tea, I meditated on a rock in the stream, then cooked breakfast, grateful for solitude and my lightweight stove. Pumping water with a filtration device, my attention was absorbed: muscles working, sounds of water. In such moments of presence, my sense of self quietly dissolved into nature.

I packed for a hike to a high peak, where vast views would unfold. I started up the trail, winding past a beaver pond and stands of white birch, absorbed in a sensory world of colors, smells, and sensations.

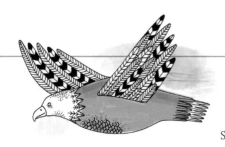

The shape of a tree reminded me of a certain yoga pose. Synapses linked the pose to a former colleague who, years earlier, had invited me to collaborate on a book about yoga. The project had soured, as his investor had backed out. But before that, I had increasingly found his personality infuriating. He had advised me on things that I had more experience with. He had pontificated. I had longed to tell him off, but never did.

The body was hiking, but the mind was deep in that long-forgotten relationship. I was flooded with judgmental opinions and agitated emotions. It went on for 20 or 30 minutes. When a hawk was startled from a tree near the trail, I reacted angrily. Where was the delight I would normally feel? Swept away. By a memory, an eruption of thoughts, and a mood, though nothing had actually happened. Suddenly I saw the comedy of it, and laughed out loud. I paused, took a deep breath, washing the mind clear. Walking again, I used my steps and breathing to guide my attention back to this step, this place.

5 THE MEDICINE OF WALKING

Before riding on animals and machines, humans walked. But in a mechanized, digital world, we're alienated from this fundamental process, and distracted by infinite options and devices. A poisonous luxury: being sedentary, overdosed in choices. *To mark this message urgent AND confidential, press five.* We walk to find ourselves again, in a new way. Walking connects us to ourselves as mammals, and to simplicity—free from a sense of self that exists only in our mind. When animals suffer pain or trauma, they heal mostly through movements, which allow them to integrate the experience and reengage with living. The key thing is they move, and so must we. Movement helps process stress through the body, whether it's the stress of being busy, a social slight that pierces the ego's self-esteem, or a serious trauma. When hurt, we may freeze, and go numb and paralyzed. We cannot stay frozen for long. To thrive, we must move, not to get anywhere, but for the medicine of movement itself.

Who Walks with Me?

When walking, the obstacle that trips us up the most is ourselves. Buddhist teacher Jack Kornfield tells of a cartoon in a magazine that illustrated the challenge of the self. It shows a single car on a desert road. At the roadside, a sign reads: "The next 200 miles: Your own tedious thoughts." The mind's default setting is thinking, overwhelmingly about ourselves, our lives, our self-image, and our concerns.

Mindful walking gives us perspective. Through the practice we slowly see these self-thoughts for what they are: a habit of the mind—less of a problem if we observe them mindfully. We don't have to take all thoughts seriously, and can see them with amusement and curiosity.

Buddhists call this the realization of "no self," the idea that our self isn't entirely real—it's mostly thoughts in the mind. Once understood, it's an enormous relief. The insecurities, fears, and doubts that emanate from the self have less power. Mindfully walking, we learn to simply be the presence that experiences the walk. We're simply walking, experiencing the joy of being "self-less" for a little while.

FORGET YOUR SELF,
LACE YOUR SHOES

As you prepare to start a mindful walk, drop into the observing mind before you even take a step. As you pick up your shoes to put them on, notice the touch of the hands to the shoes, and let the noticing mind come to the forefront of your awareness.

Allow thinking to recede into the background, and meditate as you feel your muscles engaging to hold the shoes, your spine bending as you put them on. Notice your breathing.

As you lace the shoes, take in the simplicity of these actions, doing your best not to let the mind race ahead and away from the moment. Imbue the actions of putting on the shoes with an intention to be fully present, for these details and for the moments of this day. We may say silently:

"I AM FULLY HERE,
PRESENT FOR
WHAT'S HAPPENING
NOW."

"I DON'T WANT
TO MISS A MOMENT
OF MY LIFE."

Transcending the Burden of Self

We can walk for exercise, and for something far deeper: to heal our *self*—our regrets and shame, our fear, our worries about the future. We walk to find relief from the endless doubts and opinions we have about our lives. These opinions can become a kind of mental prison, blocking us from trying new things. Through mindful walking we see that, in fact, we don't have a "life." It doesn't exist in the way we thought. "My life" is a set of ideas, memories, and fantasies—about the past, future, and an abstract self. *It exists only in the mind.* Mindfully walking, we experience being fully alive without the preoccupation of self. Our attention opens outward, first to the step, then the larger pulsation of life, the complexity of human history, and to how remarkable our planet is, floating in vast emptiness. Or perhaps just how we can help a friend.

We walk to find truth. Our fluctuating sense of self tells us that we're OK one moment, but not the next. Which narrative is right? We can spend a lifetime fending off our own critical thoughts, but it's like racing on a hamster wheel. We can never outrun them. There's ultimately no proving our worthiness, because each success can always be countered by the next "failure." We need an entirely different

medicine. Buddhist teacher Shunryu Suzuki-Roshi calls it the acceptance that "you are perfect just as you are and you could use a little improvement." Mindfully walking, we accept the walk as it is, even if there's noise, trash, or ugliness. Then we extend the acceptance to ourselves.

There's no judging, there's only the truth: "I am walking." Just for now, that's all we need to know. From that solid foundation, instead of shifting opinions, our actions are more skillful. We take a step and ask, "Now, what seems to be the right thing to do next?"

THE PRACTICE OF NON-STRUGGLE

Walking with the ease of non-struggle is our practice. Effort is necessary in walking meditation, and at times so is struggle—sometimes we have to wrestle our attention to obey. That's a productive or wise struggle. We're practicing letting go of struggle that is unproductive: struggle with things we have no influence over, like the weather, other people's opinions, or our own moods and thoughts. Wisdom reveals to us that struggle with these things just creates suffering and expends energy fruitlessly. Our practice is to settle into a state of acceptance, or non-struggle, with each mindful step.

- Find a place to walk and ask yourself if you are ready to let go of some things. To cue the letting go, scan the body before you walk and release as much unhelpful muscle tension as you can. This is often in the shoulders, arms, hands, and face.

- Start walking, noticing what's around and inside you. Acknowledge each sound, feeling, object, mood, thought, and urge. Then take your mental hands off it. "No struggle," you might say to yourself.

- Walk, and when you notice that something bothers you, say, "Hello struggle." Focus mindfully on the annoyance and reactivity in you getting activated, rather than the thing that you're struggling with. With each step, we reinforce awareness that it's the struggle reaction itself that creates misery.

- As you walk, notice how things come to disturb you. But in fact it's usually our attention that goes out to engage the visitor, marching up to the noise as if to say: "What gives you the right? Can't you see I need peace and quiet while I practice?"

- It's okay not to enjoy things that you experience, like the honking of car horns or a loud truck passing. But make a distinction: not liking or not preferring is different from struggling. Walk, and cultivate the discernment between simple not liking and struggling. Say to yourself, "Let go, let go, let go."

WHEN WE SURRENDER OUR STRUGGLE TO CONTROL THINGS WE CAN'T, WE STOP FIGHTING A NO-WIN BATTLE— AND EMERGE VICTORIOUS.

For the Benefit of All

One of the most powerful gifts of mindful walking may come through our wish that others could benefit from what the practice has given us. As our practice progresses and the benefits take root, we naturally wish to share them with others. Rather than trying to transmit what we've learned directly, we can try the Buddhist practice of setting an intention that our mindful walking be for the benefit of all people. Setting an intention imbues our actions with purpose, and brings us into fuller alignment with what's important to us.

In the intention that our practice benefits others, there is a shift from practicing for the small self (the part of us concerned only with ourselves) to practicing through the larger self, which is part of a greater web of connections. Connecting to something bigger enriches our lives. With the wish to share what's helped us, we ourselves are permeated with generosity, and receive its benefits. It's a little like compounding interest—our feeling of

> "WHEN HAPPINESS
> IS LIKED BY ME AND OTHERS
> EQUALLY, WHAT IS SO SPECIAL
> ABOUT ME THAT I SHOULD
> STRIVE AFTER HAPPINESS
> ONLY FOR MYSELF?"
>
> **—SHANTIDEVA**

generosity feeds itself. This is the power of generosity—the giver benefits in part simply through the intention of being generous.

If we find our practice brings us calm, patience, or good humor, we may pause for a moment before we walk, to set an intention that these qualities may radiate from us to anyone we meet. As we come to understand the causes, and easing, of suffering in our mindful walking, in a humble way we see that each bit of practice reduces the suffering in the world a tiny bit. In this and other ways we multiply the benefits of practice, and through the dynamics of generosity, we ourselves may receive even more than we give.

6 THE TIME IS (ALWAYS) NOW

As we have seen, walking through our apartment, a street, or remote valley, we're often not there. The mind has gone into the future, solving problems that may never exist, or the past, reengineering things long gone. We walk but don't see the landscape. This breeds attention deficit and drains satisfaction from life, leaving us empty, unsatisfied. The emptiness drives a search for some *thing* to fill it—reinforcing the belief that happiness is elsewhere, in the past or future.

Welcome to the exquisite stress of time travel. Living two lives at once, or trying to. "I'd rather be skiing," says the bumper sticker. But how often when skiing are we thinking of the hot chocolate at the end of the run? Mindful walking is the radical act of living one moment at a time, and it comes with its own bumper sticker: "I'd rather be here now."

Becoming and Being

When the needle is in the groove of mindful walking, we're moving but not trying to get anywhere. Conventionally, the purpose of walking is to get from A to B. In this practice, we may be walking to a destination, but we cultivate another purpose: getting from (A) discontent to (B) content. It's an inner journey.

This invokes a rich spiritual principle—the paradox of Becoming and Being. Although we may need to strive to accomplish many things in life (Becoming), this same striving can leave us unhappy with how things are now. Happiness can get chronically postponed, until things are the way we imagine they should be—perhaps until we lose those extra ten pounds, or make more money. This paradox can go much deeper, into existential questions, such as our life purpose. Are we here on Earth to acquire and accomplish things and prove that we're successful? If our motivation for an action is that we believe it will make us more interesting, we may feed a source of stress and suffering: a belief, often beyond our awareness, that we're not interesting enough. Such endeavors may boost our self-esteem temporarily, but ultimately they drain us.

Mindful walking cultivates a reasonable balance and interplay between these opposites. We're practicing *being* content while also striving to *become* more skillful and more able to be present. We begin to discern more wholesome goals, like becoming more helpful to our community or becoming more healthy. We feel a sense of balance, as our inner and outer purposes align. We discover a new way of simply being present for life experiences. If we take a trip to Italy, it's not about becoming a more interesting person but for the rich experiences. Walking in Tuscany, we cultivate appreciation for beauty, history, and our good fortune in visiting. With each step, we let go of Becoming and open to Being. This is the mind of stillness, contentment, inner abundance, and joy.

TAKE FIVE

THE MIND AND MUSCLE OF GRASPING

To cultivate states of ease, calm, and contentment as we walk, we tune in to the mind, but also to muscle activity throughout the body. A complex feedback loop exists between the mind, body, and nervous system. Awareness of cause and effect among these systems is the foundation of thriving in body and mind. It allows us to guide our parts to work together in harmony.

Habitual muscle tension feeds unhelpful nervous system arousal, and mind states of grasping: trying to control, avoid, or judge things in a way that's not helpful. Releasing unnecessary muscle tension is a simple way to nudge the mind to take it easy and simply be present.

Begin by standing still and closing your eyes. Next, tighten every muscle you can in the body—in your face, hands, legs, feet, etc.—and hold them squeezed tight for four or five seconds. Then release everything, and stand quietly, noticing the difference. Repeat once or twice more.

This has two benefits: It supports mindfulness, and increases your ability to notice unhelpful tension.

Slowly move into walking, bringing careful attention to the body. Focus on muscles. You'll notice muscles engaging helpfully, such as in the legs and hips. Notice places where the muscles are tight but don't need to be, like in the face or shoulders. As you move, invite these muscles to chill, or better yet, to melt. Let the shoulders and arms go limp and just hang from the torso. Let the facial muscles release any expression. Does the mind seem to relax as well?

As you walk, say to yourself:

"RELAX THE FACE."

"RELAX THE JAW."

"RELEASE THE BELLY."

"RELEASE THE SHOULDERS."

"RELEASE TENSION IN THE ARMS."

"RELEASE TENSION IN THE MIND."

"I HAVE EVERYTHING I NEED IN THIS MOMENT."

"THERE'S NO NEED TO STRUGGLE IN THIS MOMENT."

"ALL IS WELL."

Each Walk, and Each Life, is Fleeting

Walking in a forest or a city, we can lose our way, just as in the mind we can become lost inside ourselves, confused, and lose touch with what's true or with our values. Following a walking path is often easier than achieving clarity in the mind and in life. Walking in Manhattan, orientation is simple because most streets are on the grid system. But the life path and the mind have no such orderly grid. "What's the road to happiness?" we wonder. To skillfully navigate both outer and inner worlds, mindfulness establishes "right understanding," which means accurate perception.

Walking mindfully, we first establish right understanding on the physical level, by clearly focusing on a tree or a nearby taxicab. From this foundation of clear seeing, we examine more subtle levels of experience, like thoughts and moods. If we notice the thought, "This walk is going to be difficult," we know it's just a thought. Knowing thoughts as thoughts and not truths is accurate perception. We are aware that knowing this is crucial because so many thoughts are distorted and can lead us into confusion and poor decisions.

As we continue walking, right understanding makes clear the truth of impermanence—we perceive that each walk is a flow of changing experiences, one after another. This illuminates a truth about life that's easy to ignore: Nothing lasts forever—including us. Life is fleeting. As we grasp the importance of impermanence, we are led to reflect wisely on how we are living. What will be most important to devote precious time and energy to? The community? Kindness? Love? Mindful walking and right understanding help us to create a life rich with meaning, as we stay clear about what matters most to us. We notice the beauty around us as we walk, and appreciate life more completely, even when it's challenging. Our intention of walking mindfully radiates into an intention of living mindfully.

Mind of Curiosity

Walking in a familiar or entirely new place, the old dog of the mind is generally reluctant to learn new tricks. Our attention will tend to be on our own repetitive thoughts, and we can walk right past some remarkable things and not notice them.

It's a golden moment on a walk when we experience curiosity about our surroundings, because it opens the mind wide—to infinite possibilities. When we ask, "I wonder how that tree grew around that fencepost?" the mind expands, as big as the universe. It's the mind of creativity, play, innovative problem solving, and simply taking delight. It's one of the reasons companies

"HE WHO CAN

NO LONGER PAUSE TO

WONDER AND STAND

RAPT IN AWE IS AS GOOD

AS DEAD: HIS EYES

ARE CLOSED."

—ALBERT EINSTEIN

In the past few years, some inspired souls in Cambridge, Massachusetts, have been wrapping objects in public spaces with hand-knitted garments. Streetlight poles and parking meters, cocooned in little wool tubes—a celebration of silliness, or love, or art. How many people have walked past them without even noticing? I was one of them, until one day, mindfulness prevailed. I stopped, laughed, and dropped into the mind of curiosity: "What possessed someone to . . . ?"

like Google have ping-pong tables and other games in their corporate offices: to spark the mind of creative play. It boosts innovation.

As you walk, look around with curiosity. What does that bird see from up there? How do trees know to drop their leaves in the fall? How long would it take for that rock in the stream to be worn to sand by the rushing water? What did the first shoe look like? Walk, and let the mind play. Let any object you encounter be a bone for your mind's old dog to chew on, in a new way.

7 RELIEVING STRESS

We walk, in the rain, the snow, the mud, and with mosquitoes. Sometimes we walk in May, with blossoms and butterflies. Sometimes with music blasting from a passing car. They're all ideal conditions for a mindful walk. Don't let anyone tell you the weather is dreadful. In mindful walking it's simply weather. "Good weather" is dualistic thinking: good–bad, right–wrong, success–failure. These ideas are too rigid, simplistic, and judgmental for mindful walking. We're cultivating nonjudgment and acceptance in all conditions, in what's called unconditional well-being. We don't endure rain or loud noises, we experience them. This frees us from the trap of basing our happiness on conditions being just right, which means giving control of our well-being to things outside us. In mindful walking, well-being is in the mind state we cultivate, that knows, "Even as I feel rain, I am content." Unconditional well-being is the most reliable, unchanging kind of happiness. It's liberating, empowering, and the ultimate antidote to mind-made stress.

Understanding Stress

Mindful walking is a simple way to manage stress—that is, unless we make mindful walking stressful, as sometimes we can. Why on Earth would we do that? Because of confusion about what creates stress. A primary misconception is that it's caused by someone or something in the world around us—like the weather, traffic, or what so-and-so said about us. Take a deep breath before reading the next sentence. *I regret to inform you that you are the sole creator of the stress you experience.*

This sounds discouraging at first. But it's one of the liberating insights of mindfulness—that stress happens when we try to control or change things we can't, including how a mindful walk will be. Mindful walking helps us to understand how stress is created—that is, in our reactions to things—so we can create less of it.

Potential Sources of Stress

Here is a semi-serious list of experiences ripe with potential stress.

Birth—Being born is the leading cause of stress.

Wanting—Stress lies in the difference between how things are and how you want them to be. Stress is also wanting things to turn out well.

Knowing—Stress is trying to know what you cannot know and wishing you didn't know what you do know. Stress is not having enough information and it is having too much information.

Time—Ingredients to create stress: thoughts about the past and future. Aging is stressful. Resisting aging is more stressful.

Choice—Stress is having no choice. Stress is also having too many choices.

Thoughts—Stress is trying to control what others think about you and trying to control what, or how much, you think about others. Stress is realizing that most people aren't thinking about you. Stress is trying to control thinking. Mindful walking is not stressful, unless you think it is.

Stress and Freedom

Stress is a common human experience. We're bound in a web of responsibilities, demands, and constraints that we can neither fully control nor escape. Our own thoughts and emotions are often difficult. It's easy to struggle against this reality. Mindful walking is a peaceful path through the tangle of life's demands and challenges. Walking mindfully creates an inner refuge of freedom, a sense of well-being unaffected by our circumstances, what our thoughts are, or how we feel.

As we walk, we create a sense of freedom in how we carry ourselves. It's been said that certain doomed men and women have walked to their execution with their heads held high and proud, a confidence in their stride—claiming their freedom, despite their dire circumstances. Those approaching death by illness or old age can display a similar inner serenity. From a certain view, those who die in a mind state of freedom die free. But we don't wait until death approaches to claim inner well-being. We do it in each walk.

> "YOU HAVE FREEDOM
> WHEN YOU'RE EASY IN
> YOUR HARNESS."
>
> **—ROBERT FROST**

WALKING WITH FREEDOM

As you walk, bring attention to the way you're holding yourself. The posture of freedom is the beginning of a mind of freedom.

Be aware of the places that feel tight or fearful, and invite the tension to uncoil. Allow an openness, dignity, and ease into your movements, and into your breathing.

Let the opening in the body catalyze an opening in the mind, to realize freedom and dignity now, in this moment.

Don't wait until you perfect your practice of mindful walking to experience it. Feel it now, imperfect as your body, mood, life circumstances, retirement portfolio, or walk might currently be. Bring a slight smile to your lips, and notice if you can connect with a few square inches of inner freedom.

Creative Hopelessness

If we are walking with mindfulness, we are open to things as they are. We are not hoping for a good walk or a peaceful state of mind. Hoping to be peaceful, in fact, can be an enormous hindrance to mindfulness and peace. It causes frustration, as we attempt to force mindfulness to happen.

In mindful walking we let go of hope. No hope can sound dreadful. But not when we understand that sometimes hoping is trying to control things we can't, and it often creates stress and anxiety. When hoping for good weather on vacation, or hoping guests will enjoy our dinner party, we expend energy clinging to a future experience we want. That drains us, creates tension in the body, and sets up disappointment if things don't go our way. It robs us of the present moment. Mindful walking teaches that happiness isn't in getting what we want, but in the joy of relaxing into things as they are.

Mindfully walking, we're in a state of what psychotherapists call "creative hopelessness"—which allows the spontaneous creation of new insights and perspectives as we let go of hoping or trying to control. It's a flexible mind state in which we're open to being surprised. It's an inherent capacity that emerges when we're willing to relinquish habitual beliefs. Its motto might be: "Oh, I never thought of it like that before."

WALKING WITH HOPELESSNESS

Before you start a walk, affirm that you aren't seeking any special outcome; instead, set an intention to practice opening to things as they are in each moment.

As you walk, be attentive to any aspect of movement you haven't noticed before, perhaps such as the complex connections between the parts of the body involved in walking. Let your attention drift to explore the spaces around you, and allow yourself to be surprised or notice something new. Notice what this way of goal-free walking feels like mentally and emotionally.

Walking in stormy weather, we're aware that sleet and wind are not our preference. But in creative hopelessness, we're open to experiencing this weather in a new way. We discover poetry in the sound of sleet hitting our jacket. We're surprised as a harmonic riff emerges. We notice hypnotic beauty in the path slowly turning the color of grey steel. Use your mind like the sculptor Andy Goldsworthy, who creates stunning temporary artworks in natural settings, out of the rocks, twigs, ice, and petals he finds.

When not hoping for anything the mind is playing and creating, and there can be a thread of happiness—runny nose, cold toes, and all.

From Trash to Treasure

Walking along a roadside busy with cars, there's a randomly curated public exhibition. A gaze in the weeds and grass reveals cultural artifacts: beer cans, lottery tickets, cigarette butts, energy drink cans, candy bar wrappers. Not a Greenpeace pamphlet to be found, nor a long-term investment brochure. We could get mad about the mess or, like an anthropologist, wonder: "What is to be understood?" Does this collection show us that quick and cheap relief (here the temptation to quickly consume and toss remnants out of a window) has a seductive power over all of us? Or are these signs of alienation, disdain for the common good, laziness, or rebellion? Walking mindfully, we wonder, cultivating compassion for the hand that tosses, perhaps so overburdened that responsibility for one bit of trash seems too much to bear. In mindful walking, many questions, and insights, can emerge.

Consider sidewalks and walking paths—what does their presence (or lack thereof) tell us? Whether walking is valued or thought unfeasible? Where walking paths sprout, walkers come out of the woodwork (or their cars). Many cities are now honoring walking anew. Pedestrian zones fill Times Square, and to the High Line—a walking path on old rail tracks over New York—visitors flock. What does this reveal? Perhaps a thirst for the rarest treasure, and one that's not for sale: a walk.

Walking the Questions

What does it say about a culture like Switzerland's that they maintain signs for walking paths in every hamlet and town, including their largest city, Zurich? What do ubiquitous "No Trespassing" signs around private land in the U.S. reveal? What about the countless walking paths in the Czech Republic, where the foot traveler pitches a tent freely overnight? And by contrast, what can I understand from my encounter with an agitated American who scolded me and my wife for parking our car on a public road so that we could walk in the beautiful countryside? He assumed our car meant something criminal was afoot, but it was only walking afoot. Mindfully, we walk the questions.

(8) A PATH WELL CHOSEN

Mindful walking is a path of paradoxes: we walk with purpose, but not to get anywhere; we cultivate freedom, though are bound by circumstances; we make an effort to be mindful, yet already possess mindfulness. In surrendering to what unfolds, we emerge the winner: we fully accept ourselves, and notice ways we can grow and develop.

In mindful walking we are traversing what Zen Buddhists call the "razor's edge": the slim territory of paradox, where opposing truths come together. It's been said that a paradox is the highest achievement of human thought—where opposing ideas can both be true and together reveal a greater truth. With each mindful step we walk this tightrope of paradoxes. But there's nothing to fear in falling off. We simply step back on and resume walking.

One paradox of our practice is that each time we walk, we choose to be "choiceless." This reveals a new and liberating perspective on choices.

A Practice and a Path

We may walk the same well-worn route many times, but mindfulness prevents thoughts from leading us down a path of unhelpful thinking again and again. If we allow our thoughts to go unobserved, they may lead us into a tangle of worries and woe. Just as a path well trodden wears a rut in the land, habitual thoughts wear a rut in the mind. Neuroscientists have a saying about this: "What fires together, wires together." It means that when two ideas frequently link, a well-established pathway, known as a synapse, forms in the brain. If a thought about "my life" is frequently followed by "not measuring up," a synapse is established, and that gives the ring of truth to this self-view, as the former inevitably connects to the latter. If instead, "so grateful to be alive" is linked with "my life," a very different connection grows. This is a key idea of neuroplasticity, the study of how we literally both shape the mind with mental habits and have a choice about the shape it will take.

About 2,500 years before the birth of modern neuroscience, the Buddha expressed this in a frequently cited teaching:

> "WHATEVER
> THE MIND FREQUENTLY
> DWELLS UPON BECOMES
> THE INCLINATION
> OF THE MIND."
>
> —THE BUDDHA

As we understand the power thoughts and mental reactions wield over our lives, we grasp the role mindfulness can have in shaping our destiny. We come to see the possibility of mindfulness as a life path, a methodology we can draw on in any life situation. We use mindfulness, when walking and otherwise, to observe repetitive thoughts and how they underpin habitual views. We investigate whether mindfulness supports us to feel, behave, or think differently. Then we must choose—to be mindful, or to passively allow unhelpful thoughts to shape us. Mindfully walking, our practice is a chosen path—not just the one with the deepest rut.

Choiceless Awareness

Walking into a neighborhood that we find ugly, we may close a door inside ourselves, rejecting what we encounter. In mindful walking, we stay open instead and just notice: "this pleases me—and this, less so." We notice what displeasure feels like, what ugliness feels like, what beauty feels like. This is the path of being fully alive. We don't resist or judge anything, or block anything from our awareness. Our practice is to engage with the full spectrum of experience. We are free to roam anywhere—the five-star hotel, sacred temple, cemetery, and dive bar. In each, we are equally at ease. There's nothing to resist.

The way we treat a mindful walk should mirror the way we treat ourselves. Our purpose is to know the whole self—not to deny anything that's real. Buddhist writer Pema Chödrön is the sage of this perspective, encouraging us to explore "the places that scare you." We notice with compassion whatever we see in our behavior, character, and thoughts.

This doesn't mean we don't govern our behavior or hold ourselves accountable. We do. But we see without censoring. Looking honestly and courageously at ourselves, we see our strengths and weaknesses, without choosing. This is known as "choiceless awareness."

"I DESTROY MY ENEMIES BY MAKING THEM MY FRIENDS."

—ABRAHAM LINCOLN

TAKE FIVE) NOTICING INTERNAL STATES

In this practice, walk slowly and closely observe your changing thoughts and feelings to gain a clearer understanding of the fleeting, variable nature of internal states. Here is an example of what one might notice and reflect on.

In this moment, I notice a jealous thought.

In this moment, I notice fear.

In this moment, I feel generous and kind.

Now, I notice irritation and impatience.

Now, I notice I'm skillful.

Now, I notice I'm unskillful.

Which am I? Kind? Unkind? Skillful? Unskillful?

Am I a good person or a bad one?

I am none of these.

I am the mindful, compassionate presence knowing each changing state.

TAKE FIVE

FREEING OURSELVES FROM THOUGHTS

Many a mindful walker has lamented walks being "ruined" by persistent distracting thoughts, which descended like a plague of locusts. Usually the walker, having pulled over to page through their mental handbook, tried every mindfulness technique they knew with increasing intensity, attempting to defeat the thoughts. This is a fool's errand, because the mind produces thoughts like the tabloids produce drama. There's no stopping them. Our goal is to free ourselves from struggling with them.

In mindful walking, we can view thoughts like birds flying through the sky. As we walk, we make a choice to let them be. We affirm that we are the bird-watcher, not the bird. As we choose not to engage with the thoughts, we notice if this brings a sense of freedom. Thoughts are not our problem to solve or even understand.

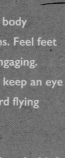

- As you walk, bring mindfulness to your body and notice sensations. Feel feet touching, muscles engaging. Mindful of the body, keep an eye out for a thought-bird flying through the mind.

- Once you notice a thought-bird, bring attention back to the body. Affirm that you are the mindful observer of each sensation, and each thought.

- Notice sensation in the knee, then a thought in the mind—but stay in your position as the observer. Don't get drawn in to what the thought is about.

We have no choice about what thoughts appear, but we can choose just to notice and not engage with them. It's like the difference between witnessing an argument and getting drawn into participating in it. We stay the witness.

As you walk and practice, allowing thoughts to float by, notice how the practice makes you feel.

Holding Steady

Mindfully walking, we can cultivate steadiness both on
the walking path and the life path. The seed of
steadiness blossoms into non-reactivity amid the
inevitable flow of opposites all humans
experience—praise and blame, gain and loss,
sickness and health, pain and pleasure. This is the
messy process of cultivating wisdom—the capacity to
recognize what we can and can't control, and act accordingly.
Our practice frees us from the bind of reacting to what provokes us.
We are not swayed by each itch, urge, or frustration. We might waver
and weave, but we hold to the path.

PRAISE   GAIN   HEALTH   PLEASURE

BLAME   LOSS   SICKNESS   PAIN

The Call of the Marshmallow

Since the 1960s, cognitive researchers have used marshmallows to assess young children's abilities to resist immediate gratification in favor of long-term reward. In Walter Mischel's classic experiment, each child is offered either one sweet now or two later if they can resist eating the first for a little while. The child is then left alone with the single marshmallow. A camera records the children as they struggle and squirm. A miniature opera unfolds: will the child stay steady when pulled by desire? Follow-ups to these studies have found that a child's capacity to postpone pleasure and tolerate distress is linked to success in later life. We strengthen this same muscle in each walk.

Mindful walking is a journey into ourselves, through the muddy landscape of our moods, wounds, fears, and agitations. Demons arise to harass us, and our practice holds the fortitude to face them. We know not to battle them—we simply bear witness. There is an alchemy that happens when we can look our demons in the eye. Their dark, heavy power to hinder or destroy us is transformed as we simply meet their gaze. To our surprise, as we hold steady enough, our demons can bestow blessings; they catalyze our resilience. Lead turns to gold.

(9) WALKING IN NATURE

Walking in natural places affects us differently than moving through man-made surroundings. A forest or meadow untouched by human design plugs into something uncomplicated in the mind and heart. They speak to us, not in words or ideas, but by reflecting something in us we've forgotten: simple presence. They invite mindfulness—simply being aware, without thinking, planning, or worrying. They cue us to look and see differently—with openness, wonder, and the curiosity of a child. Encountering a tree, if we're mindful, we perceive its essence, its unselfconscious *treeness*. It's not trying to please us, and isn't wishing it were somewhere else, doing something else. Each tree, hill, weed, and bumblebee, being just what it is, can be a mentor, guiding us to discover our own essential nature: just movement, breath, and awareness. Mindfully walking, we're simply being what we are, doing what we do, noticing what we notice.

Flowing with the Go

Walking in a natural place, we can use the rich details of our surroundings to cultivate mindful attention. As we walk, we direct our focus toward the shapes and textures of the path, the colors of foliage, the feeling of wind or sun on the skin. We guide the mind toward becoming absorbed in each sensory element we encounter, lingering on it, noticing each aspect of shape, light and shadow, color, sound, sensation, and smell.

As we move, we notice that the places we encounter morph and change shape as our perspective changes. In this way we experience not fixed things but a flow of sensory input, constantly shifting, new impressions emerging as others fade and disappear. The moss-covered boulder becomes a stream of changing images as we see it anew with each step. Standing still to notice a scene in front of us, here too we perceive the pulsation of life, as the light shifts, leaves move in the breeze, and clouds amble overhead.

LET AWARENESS BE AN UNCHANGING STILL POINT . . .

This parade of ever-changing experiences reflects the reality of impermanence—the changing nature of life and the world. Finding balance in the flow of life changes, going with the flow rather than resisting it, is one of the main principles of

. . . OBSERVING THE FLOW OF CONSTANT CHANGES.

mindfulness. Our practice also helps us to see how we create stress by expecting people and things to stay the same and becoming frustrated when they change. Mindfulness, on the other hand, is finding stability in the steady awareness that watches the flow.

A rushing stream, or the sounds of the wind, are ideal objects of mindfulness and impermanence. Bringing attention to the sound of rushing water, we perceive it isn't a single sound, but an unfolding chain of sounds. From one perspective the stream is a thing; from another, a process. Mindfully observing, we take in this paradox, allowing it to enrich our experience of our walk and our life.

Walking Small Amid the Grand

SHARING MOMENTS

Where the vastness of the planet reveals itself, walking is a powerful experience, more so if the mind is present. Walks in the Sierra, Rockies, and Himalayas have shaped me in ways that are hard to quantify. Taking in the magnitude of these wild places, each just a chunk of the Earth, perspective on human incarnation shifts. Walking, we experience how long it takes to traverse even a sliver of the vastness. The difference in scale between a human body and the body of the planet is revealed in each step. Our conventional view is dislodged. We see the world and our "problems" in a different light.

In the Ticinese mountains in Switzerland, a wild, sleepy backwater in the Alps, my wife and I took a wrong turn. We had set out from the exquisite mountain *capanna*, or hut, to cross a steep, short route of perhaps 9 miles. It was supposed to be a walk over a little toe of the beast. Instead, we tumbled deep into the belly. Crossing a high pass by a snowy route, I misread the map, sending us off course. It took hours to realize my mistake. By then, we were committed to crossing a huge rockfall, an unthinkably immense pile of boulders.

Stepping from one boulder to the next in a trance, we knew crossing was our only chance of finding a trail marker. Each new horizon showed only more boulders. The mind could not digest the scale of it.

It was impossible to overlook: we were tiny and relatively powerless in this vast place. It was fascinating, thrilling, and frightening. Sobering, like a question that kept asking: "What's most important in this life?" It's one of the many gifts of crossing great wild areas on foot: known references and the illusion of control are stripped away. If we walk with mindfulness, it's an invaluable chance to look in the mirror and reflect on how one is living.

Connecting to Nature

With mindful walking, we know we're doing more than just moving our feet. We're purifying the mind of unhelpful patterns, a step at a time. Each step liberates us from the past (some Buddhists call this "purifying karma"). With every stride, if we are present and engaged, we also create something new. Like placing a little pebble on a pile, each mindful step accumulates inner presence. Over time the pebbles form a mound, someday a mountain. The steady, mountain-like nature in us is called equanimity. Make it part of your practice to affirm this cleansing–creating effect in each step.

As we walk in nature, we can draw on archetypes we see—trees that are tall but rooted; a vast and open sky, unharmed by storms; water that flows easily around obstacles—to inspire and shape our character. Invoking elements of nature reminds us that we are of nature: creatures nurtured by the Earth and deeply connected to its natural intelligence and resilience.

TAKE FIVE — NATURE, IN A FEW WORDS

As you walk, try a simple mantra to invoke elements of nature and emphasize your nature connection:

"WALKING, I FLOW
EASILY AROUND OBSTACLES.

AS I AM MOVING, I CARRY
STILLNESS IN ME.

THERE IS PLENTY OF SPACE INSIDE ME
FOR ANYTHING I MIGHT FEEL.

I AM MOVING FORWARD, KNOWING I AM
ALREADY WHERE I NEED TO BE.

I ACCEPT EACH MOMENT AND
EACH STEP AS IT IS."

As you walk, be aware of what's moving—the body, people around you, birds flying, cars driving. Bring attention to the qualities inside that you are cultivating, the inner resilience of the tree, stream, sky, or mountain. The mind is drawn to this rich presence inside, and soothed by it, even when you're surrounded by busy and noisy activity. This is your inner resource, and it is always with you, to connect to wherever you go.

THE RADIANCE OF EMPTY SPACE

In some Buddhist teachings, the mind is defined as emptiness itself. Thoughts and sensory impressions occur in that empty space, and awareness is there, witnessing each one. Conventionally an empty space may be considered sad, but in the Buddhist view it is neutral, radiant, free of troubles. In this practice, we'll explore this perspective and notice how it affects us.

Find a peaceful natural setting and begin by standing in a place in which you can pause for a few moments. Close your eyes and firmly root your feet, unlocking the knees slightly to engage the leg muscles. Hold the body upright but not rigid. Soften the shoulders, arms, and hands. Invite any muscle tension in the face to soften. Allow the belly and ribcage to be flexible and responsive, expanding and contracting as the breath comes in and out.

"I KEEP MY MIND AS EMPTY AS POSSIBLE. THAT WAY, BEAUTY CAN COME IN."

—YOKO ONO

Imagine or visualize that the inside of the body is an open, uncluttered, and infinitely spacious place. Invite the breath to flow fully in to that space. Breathe in a relaxed but full way, expanding and contracting the torso, not straining. Focus on experiencing your body as spacious inside.

Slowly open your eyes, keeping awareness focused on the inner space by keeping your eyes unfocused. Slowly begin to step, as you keep the breath flowing fully. As each sensory experience happens—the sensations of stepping, the seeing of objects, hearing of sounds—imagine each one being received into the empty space inside, where it is fully known and absorbed. Think of yourself as both the empty space and the awareness that notices what is received there. Try not to form an opinion about anything that's received, focusing on being neutral space, like the air that receives the falling raindrop without opinion.

Pause, stand still, and notice how the practice affected you. Remember that you can return to this spaciousness anytime, by softening around the ribs, breathing fully, and bringing your attention to the space inside.

10 WALKING MINDFULLY IN THE CITY

It can feel quite lonely and isolated walking mindfully in a city or other busy place. You might feel like you're the only person within a thousand miles who is even slightly interested in meditation. Surrounded by cascades of frenetic activity, your mindful walk can feel like a drop of water in an ocean of craziness. You may become discouraged or doubtful. Thoughts tell you you're making a fool of yourself, or wasting your time. This is an encounter with the hindrances, the obstacles that inevitably arise in practicing mindfulness (see page 124). Such difficulties on the path are symbolized by mud or manure, and mindfulness practitioners teach that the lotus blossom—freedom, well-being, and happiness—blooms in this mud. As Buddhist monk Thich Nhat Nanh says, "No mud, no lotus." With growing wisdom, we meet the obstacles we encounter in hectic urban spaces with a knowing smile, understanding that if we don't struggle in response, each obstacle reinforces our inner well-being.

Riding Waves in the City

Walking in an urban environment, a flood of sounds, sights, and smells washes over us. As traffic rushes past, we nearly collide with a man walking toward us, his eyes glued to a mobile device. Our mind is fragmented, and it's easy to become irritated. Sometimes it feels like the uproar will curl the hair.

These are perfect conditions for mindful walking. We don't need the serenity of a temple to practice. As we have seen, a key part of mindfulness is letting go of resistance and trying to control—recognizing that often there's no way to bring quiet and order to what's going on around us. Frenetic surroundings don't have to jolt us into internal chaos. Our practice is finding the eye of the hurricane, inside ourselves.

Feeling Moved

To be the witness is to be present and attentive without struggling, reacting, or fighting—but we do not become uncaring. We may be greatly moved by beauty, or tragedy, or ugliness on our walk through streets or a city park, but we don't get swept away by reacting to the tumult or trying to subdue it.

"YOU CAN'T STOP THE WAVES, BUT YOU CAN LEARN TO SURF."

—PROFESSOR JON KABAT-ZINN, CREATOR OF THE MINDFULNESS-BASED STRESS REDUCTION PROGRAM

Our breath leads us to a steady place inside. Bringing attention to each inhale, we drop into the non-reactive observer in us, the part of the mind that's just witnessing the waves crashing over us.

As we walk mindfully through hectic streets, we coach ourselves to let go and allow things to be, whether we enjoy what we meet or not. We let it all wash over us—including our reactions—feeling what we feel, riding the waves of experience.

Walking Mindfully in the City

FOCUS AND ATTENTION IN A BUSY SPACE

TAKE FIVE

Each moment we're walking in a city, we're receiving reams of sensory input to sort through. Even sitting in a quiet room, or walking in a harmonious meadow, there's a fire hose of sights, sounds, smells, and sensations to contend with. And then there are our non-stop thoughts. It's no surprise attention and focus are challenging. To avoid being endlessly distracted, we learn to manage less the input and more where we put our attention. This simple mindful walking practice illustrates this.

Begin a slow, steady walk, aware of all the things that vie for your attention through each of the senses. Notice that thoughts frequently appear too. Walk for a moment or two, making no effort to control your attention. Let it just drift from one thing to the next. Have compassion for yourself and others—the cornucopia of distractions is formidable and the untrained mind is helpless as a baby.

Then begin to direct attention to your feet, focusing on how each step feels. Notice not just the step itself, but the qualities of it. Is it comfortable or uncomfortable? Is the contact with the ground soft or hard? Notice carefully the sensations and movements of the feet stepping, without adding words in your mind. Expect your focus to be unsteady, with thoughts frequently distracting you. Turn back to the feet each time you've lost focus.

Now begin to add the words "Right here" and "Right now" as each foot makes contact with the ground. This occupies the thinking mind—and beats it at its own game. Walk, repeat the words, and be aware of things getting simpler. There will still be lots of background noise, including your own thoughts. No worries. You don't need to eliminate the sources of chatter and distraction. Rather, you're practicing a habit of simplicity and focus in your mind's foreground. The background will always be busy. Control of attention comes through consciously choosing what's in the foreground.

RIGHT HERE

RIGHT NOW

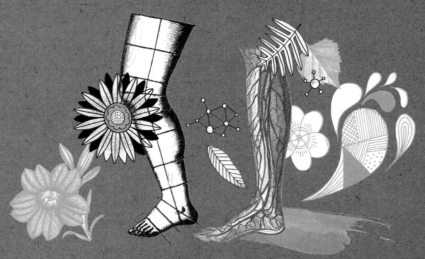

TETHERED TO SIMPLICITY

One of the first goals of mindful walking is to steady the mind to create a sense of stability inside. Walking in a busy or urban place, this can be especially hard. Try using simple cognitive cues to help create a pattern of internal simplicity and mindfulness.

Since busy places can overstimulate us and get our attention bouncing wildly from one thing to the next, we are going to use another simple series of words to occupy the thinking mind just enough that it can't run off too far on a tangent. It's one of the reasons many religious traditions use prayer recitation or mantras—to focus, steady, and purify the mind. We'll borrow from that tradition in this practice, and add a five-word phrase developed by the Kripalu school of yoga.

BREATHE

RELAX

- As you begin your mindful walk, invite the body to be upright— firmly engaged but still relaxed and flexible.

- Make your movements as smooth, balanced, and unhurried as you're able without trying too hard. Move with ease and grace.

- Allow your attention to drift outward to take in your surroundings, but stay attuned to the body, checking back every few moments to notice movements.

- Once you're moving in a reasonably balanced way and are flowing between noticing the external and the internal, add a simple phrase to invite simplicity in the mind. As you walk, silently say "Breathe, relax," with each step or two. The "relax" is a cue to let go of any unhelpful muscle tension, like tightness in the face, hands, or shoulders.

- Continue walking, and try lengthening the phrase to "Breathe, relax, feel, watch, allow," over five or ten, or more, steps. Let the phrase be a thread to which you stay loosely tethered as you walk. Its repetitive nature invites a trancelike experience, but one in which we're present, attentive, content, and at ease.

FEEL   WATCH   ALLOW

The Mundane to the Mystical

One of the gifts of mindful walking is the bridge it can create between the mundane and the mystical. As the mind grows more contemplative, we investigate things around us with new curiosity. Learning to observe thoughts, we hold our self-concerns with more perspective and experience our "self" as something greater (or perhaps lesser): presence or empty space itself. As a taste unfolds on the tongue, we know our self as simply the awareness in which the taste is experienced. Sounds come to our ears, and we're the awareness through which sounds are experienced.

As mindfulness attunes us to cause and effect, we see connections all around with new eyes. Walking through a city, we're more aware that we inhale the oxygen that the trees lining the streets exhale; we're conscious of the fact that in farms out of town the soil's nutrients feed plants which feed us; we understand the passing truck carries our food to the supermarket, and that everything we purchase there will end up back in the planet. We've known this intellectually

> "IT REQUIRES
> A VERY UNUSUAL MIND
> TO UNDERTAKE THE
> ANALYSIS OF THE OBVIOUS."
>
> —PROFESSOR ALFRED
> NORTH WHITEHEAD

before, but awareness of this interconnectedness now starts to become more of an intuitive, lived experience.

Our view of the body also begins to evolve. Catching a glimpse of our face reflected in a store window, we no longer take the face so literally as who we are. Looking more deeply, we see it merely as wrapping paper. We're not the face or skin, any more than we are the intestines or kidneys. The body is not who we are, *we're in* the body. With a sense of wonder, we experience our consciousness animating our body—we see our body as the lantern holding the candle. And as we're increasingly aware of the interconnectedness of life forms on the planet, we may wonder if our own conscious mind shares a source with the intelligence of the flower that somehow knows to turn toward the sun. In mindful walking, these questions simply arise of their own accord. You don't even need Pink Floyd on your iPod to take you there.

11 MINDFUL WALKING IN EVERYDAY LIFE

As mindful walking becomes more familiar, we create moments of practice in everyday places, like when stepping from the desk to the photocopy machine. A few brief steps of attentive awareness reinforce the mindful approach for encounters with coworkers, our children, our partner, or other interactions in which we need to be skillful. Mindful walking transitions from an exotic thing done in special meditative experiences to something woven into the daily routine.

These miniature mindful walks in your home, office, in stores, and other places lets the power of mindfulness go viral. We notice the observing mind in the background wherever we go, and little miracles happen. Old patterns of behavior don't happen as automatically as before. Small but important victories occur, in which we don't take the bait and we ignore an urge that would normally rule us. A thread of awareness is now present in more encounters, and increasingly we're able to choose rather than react.

Emotional Rescue

On each mindful walk, we meet someone on the path: ourselves. Each moment of practice sees us develop a new kind of self-attunement. As we pay close attention to the experiences unfolding in the mind and body, we foster intimacy with ourselves. This has a very practical benefit: we become increasingly able to recognize stress and agitation starting to smolder inside before it reaches full-strength adrenaline conflagration. We detect a wisp of smoke and know a fire is in the making, and use this as a signal to practice. We don't wait until the house is in flames. Think of mindful walking as emotional rescue (in the words of the Stones)—a practice we use when we're hanging by a thread off

an emotional cliff. And as our self-awareness grows, we can identify places and situations we know are frequently challenging or likely to be so, and can plan ahead to bring awareness into those settings. It's like boosting your immunity to stress by taking a mindfulness supplement.

Outside the staff meeting room for the manager, the ICU unit for the nurse, the classroom aisles for the high-school teacher, or the bedroom hallway for the parent of teenagers—anywhere conflict and pressure are likely to arise, mindfulness can be drawn upon. One parent of a teen describes a practice of walking mindfully in place with his legs under the dinner table during intense family moments, when actual walking isn't an option. A woman who struggles with overeating uses mindful walking in the aisles of the supermarket, to help her make wise choices. Many professional athletes, performers, and executives are leveraging the steadying influence of mindfulness practices.

Consider where your pressure vortexes are, and plan to use mindful walking there to bring a little patience, compassion, and perspective to yourself in challenging moments. Your students, children, and coworkers will silently thank you—as will your adrenal glands.

ROUTINES OF MINDFUL WALKING

Take a moment to reflect on places you frequently walk through.
Make a list of five to ten places: from home to the metro; from your
parking spot to the office door; from the dining room to the kitchen.
If you take the time to write them down, it will help establish a link
between these places and mindful walking practice.

Now review your list of places and, for each one, close your eyes
for a few moments and imagine yourself walking mindfully there.
Visualize yourself hurrying to the metro, and *feel what it will feel like* as
you drop into a content, spacious, observing state during the walk.

Generate those feelings in your body now, as you imagine this moment
of mindfulness on the sidewalk. (This will generate a kind of placebo
effect.) As you suspend disbelief for this exercise, make the experience
of having a peaceful mind state, and the pleasant feelings that you'd
like to come with it, as real as possible.

On some level, your body will experience this as real, as when someone is given a sugar pill but is told it's medication. Studies have shown again and again that the body often reacts as if something is real if we think it's real. That's why a scary thought about a large, poisonous spider elicits feelings of revulsion—the body reacts as if the imagined situation is real. Here, an experience of peacefulness becomes real, and we link it to the place you walk. It makes mindfulness, and those feelings, more accessible on your next walk.

You don't have to do all the work of integrating mindful walking into your wider life. The places on your list will now support you. You've imbued them with mindful awareness and good feelings, and you're unlikely to walk them again unconsciously.

It just takes a little remembering:

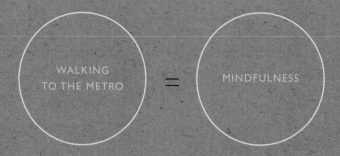

WALKING TO THE METRO = MINDFULNESS

LABELING THE FIVE HINDRANCES

An important bit of information to bring on any mindful walk is about the obstacles we unavoidably meet. There are five common ones, called the five hindrances:

DESIRE (WANTING PLEASURE)

AVERSION (DISLIKE OF WHAT'S UNPLEASANT)

DOUBT (JUDGING THOUGHTS WHICH UNDERMINE PRACTICE)

HEAVINESS AND DULLNESS (HEAVINESS OF BODY, DULLNESS OF MIND)

RESTLESSNESS (AGITATION THAT MAKES PRACTICE DIFFICULT)

The simplest way not to be swept away by these hindrances is to label them clearly. The labeling solidifies mindfulness.

Imagine walking mindfully on a summer day in a park. All is well, until you notice someone eating ice cream. Desire grips you—you haven't had dessert in too long. *Can't I just relax with a treat and not work so hard on mindful walking?* Imagine placing a small sticky note on the feeling of wanting, which says simply, "Desire."

Continuing, you meet a group of people smoking cigarettes and talking loudly. The smoke and noise disturbs you. *Do they really have to be here, now? So annoying!* Create a sticker and apply it: "Aversion." You're not quite so fully in its grip now.

On another walk, thoughts calling the value of practice into question keep looping. *I've got more important things to do, like getting things done. This mindful walking is preventing me from taking action.* But you smell a rat, and grab your sticky: "Doubt."

On other days, the walk just feels tiresome, like slogging though mud. The body is heavy and the mind lifeless. It feels like too much effort. *I can't do it anymore!* The dramatic tone of thought catches your mindful observer, and a "Heaviness and Dullness" sticky is applied.

At other times you're beset by agitation, wanting to escape at all costs, crawling out of your skin. You label it and remember just to feel. *This is what restlessness feels like,* you say quietly inside.

In the Clutches of Craving

When walking the slippery tightrope of desire—for example, the path to the refrigerator—even a few seconds of mindful awareness can help us to realize that we are on a collision course. Taking mindful steps as we approach the gates of nirvana, the noticing brain switches on. We are better able to assess the accuracy of thoughts that insist, "Must have ice cream now!" A little mindfulness

Fighting Addiction

There is a growing body of behavioral research on the positive effects of mindfulness-based approaches to craving and addiction. Mindful walking strengthens capacities that researchers believe are helpful in understanding and overcoming addiction, including:

EXPERIENTIAL ENGAGEMENT—the willingness to remain in contact with unpleasant thoughts, feelings, and experiences, rather than avoiding them through addictive substances or addictive behaviors, such as compulsively checking your email.

AWARENESS AND ACCEPTANCE—of thoughts, feelings, and sensations as they arise, without trying to alter or suppress them.

when walking to the fridge provides just enough objectivity to discern whether survival does, in fact, depend on fulfilling our desire immediately, as the craving would have us believe.

Some brain researchers refer to this effect of mindfulness as mixing some cool brain into the hot brain. MRI studies demonstrate brain areas associated with clear perception and skillfulness activate during mindfulness, balancing the urgency of reactive brain functions.

NONJUDGMENTAL PERCEPTION—viewing discomfort and ourselves with less judgment, which reduces emotional reactivity.

COMPASSION—the capacity to bring loving attention to our own distress. This is part of learning to self-soothe in healthier ways.

RECOGNITION OF IMPERMANENCE—knowing cravings are temporary and allowing them to come and go without responding.

INSIGHT INTO CAUSE AND EFFECT—recognizing destructive and futile aspects of behavior patterns, rather than denying them.

AN INTERNAL SOURCE OF WELL-BEING—instead of seeking affirmation or distraction externally, which underpins addiction.

12 MAINTAINING MINDFULNESS

For mindful walking and its benefits to flourish in your life, you'll need to nurture a lifestyle that's conducive to contemplative practice. These days, the primary challenge is creating a moderate relationship with electronic devices, so that you're using them without them using you. Digital devices tend to work at cross-purposes with being mindful—with their endless menus and options, which feed the mind's tendency to consume and wander. There's no need to throw away all your devices, delete social media accounts, and become a burlap-wearing monk. The goal is to engage wisely, enjoying their benefits but knowing their limitations and challenges too. To successfully integrate mindful walking into your routines, it may help to find regular times to turn off devices, if only for short periods. Going off the digital grid for even a small amount of time can feel challenging, but it brings the reward of a balanced mind and moderate lifestyle—what the Buddha called the "Middle Path."

The Little Things of a Big Thing

Maintaining a lifestyle that supports self-awareness and mindfulness happens, or not, in the small things we do. Compassionately but honestly, examine your habits and choices, identifying what feeds distraction and unnecessary multitasking. Reflect on your relationships with caffeine, sugar, and alcohol, and whether they play a role in avoiding being entirely present. There's no requirement to give up these intoxicants, but mindfulness will be supported by using them in moderation. Our electronic devices can also have a drug-like quality. Examine your relationship with them, including whether you frequently use a device while driving, shopping, eating a meal, or talking with people. To examine such habits requires, and supports, flexibility of mind, and builds the capacity to look deeply and perceive cause and effect in relationships—some of the key skills of mindfulness. It's also part of cultivating a lifestyle of awareness and wise relationships.

TAKE FIVE — MINDFUL LIVING, BIT BY BIT

To support being present, try the following:

- Eat breakfast without listening to the radio or looking at a device.

- One day a week or month, skip your usual cup of coffee, tea, or alcoholic drink.

- Before starting to eat, pause for 10–15 seconds to appreciate the food and invoke mindfulness in eating.

- Drive a few minutes in your car or on the bus before switching on the radio or device.

- Go for a walk without your phone.

- Leave your phone in the car or silence it when shopping.

- Don't bring electronic devices to the dinner table; light a candle instead, to symbolize a natural, steady presence. Notice what the food tastes like and discuss it with your fellow diners.

- Wonder about something without immediately searching for the answer online.

- Navigate a short trip by memory or map rather than voice-prompted GPS directions.

- Preparing a meal, use the activities of chopping, measuring, and cooking as opportunities for mindful awareness.

These little things, done repeatedly, become a big thing in one's life.

The Practice of Cultivating Wisdom

Wisdom is the result of the three progressive stages of meditation (see page 46), and it becomes a rewarding aspect of our ongoing practice of mindful walking. Buddhist teacher Jack Kornfield writes, "When we shift attention from experience to spacious consciousness that knows, wisdom arises." To do this, we bring attention to the *spacious nature of the observing mind itself.* This spaciousness is the quality of the mind that's like the vast sky through which birds, weather, and other objects move. Like the sky, it's an undisturbed and limitless presence in the mind. Connecting to it, we are knowing the mind in its ideal qualities—open, non-grasping, nonjudgmental.

Wisdom is the natural by-product of bringing awareness to this spaciousness. It's not to be confused with knowledge or arrogance, and we don't think of it as "my wisdom"—that would be an ego trip. We humbly experience it as an inherent gift of the mind that has become increasingly balanced and clear through mindfulness practice.

Once we get a glimpse of wisdom, we bring attention to it frequently, as a growing source of insight and perspective. When facing life challenges for which there is no ready solution, we often feel solace by releasing the problem into the spaciousness of the observing mind, knowing that simply regarding the problem with wisdom is the best way to hold it skillfully for now.

OBSERVING WITH WISDOM

Call to mind a life difficulty for which there is no current resolution, such as a friend who has become distant and uncommunicative.

- Close your eyes, breathe slowly, and soften your face and shoulders.

- Bring attention to the open, abundant quality of your mind, which is like a large, empty vessel.

- Imagine releasing the difficult issue into this space, gently placing it there in your mind. There is no shortage of space for the problem to settle into.

- Allow the wisdom in your mind to observe it calmly, knowing there is nothing to do with it for now but witness it and allow it to be what it is.

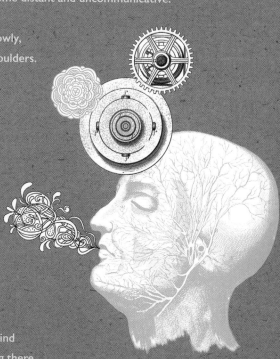

The Stuff of Mindful Living

The habits of mindful walking and mindful living are largely cognitive—internal and invisible. One of the challenges when trying to make the practice consistent is the rather intangible nature of it—it happens in the head. At times we may not be sure if we're mindful or not when walking. Other times, we may simply forget the practice. One way to address this is to create concrete reminders of the practice, and the mindful state we're cultivating.

The symbols, trinkets, and tchotchkes of mindfulness are frequently misappropriated as tacky clichés. There is a restaurant in Pennsylvania, with huge Buddha statues at the entrance, called "Buddha Martini Bar." Talk about a paradox! Visiting India one can't miss the ubiquitous signs of contemplative practice, devotion, and spirituality in the public domain. Each tiny three-wheeled taxi has a miniature altar, usually with burning incense, on the dashboard. Images of spirituality and depictions

of deities are nearly everywhere. *Stupa* structures, representing Buddha-like consciousness, appear in many vistas even in remote mountain areas. They are all reminders of practice, there to support whoever sees them.

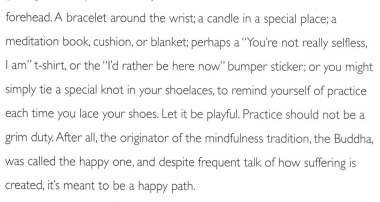

You can support your practice with similar visible reminders without building a temple in your front yard or getting a third-eye tattoo on your forehead. A bracelet around the wrist; a candle in a special place; a meditation book, cushion, or blanket; perhaps a "You're not really selfless, I am" t-shirt, or the "I'd rather be here now" bumper sticker; or you might simply tie a special knot in your shoelaces, to remind yourself of practice each time you lace your shoes. Let it be playful. Practice should not be a grim duty. After all, the originator of the mindfulness tradition, the Buddha, was called the happy one, and despite frequent talk of how suffering is created, it's meant to be a happy path.

The Three Refuges on the Path

Even though mindfulness is currently enjoying what Andy Warhol called 15 minutes of fame, perhaps even hipness, the path of mindful walking and a contemplative lifestyle can sometimes still be a lonely one. The practice flies in the face of what much of Western culture tells us is the path to happiness, and we can feel like we're swimming against the stream. It's all too easy to head out for some mindful walking and find yourself in line at Starbucks, taking the short and sweet route to happiness. In many ways the backbone of the practice is the willingness to stay engaged with things that are uncomfortable, and that's not easy. It's even harder to try to do it in isolation.

Since it's not an entirely easy path, we need support along the way. Mindfulness teachings point us to three main sources of support, sometimes called the refuges. We'll call these awareness, truth, and community. When discouragement, doubt, laziness, or the seductive song of the Grande Latte strikes, we seek refuge in the three supports:

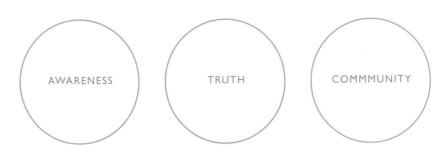

AWARENESS   TRUTH   COMMMUNITY

The Three Supports

AWARENESS: We take support from the clear, steady, open awareness that is inherent in the mind. This means we connect to the wisdom, spaciousness, ease, and compassion that our own mindful nature provides.

TRUTH: Also known as "the way," this refers to the truths of teachings on how the mind works—about how suffering is created and what brings happiness, well-being, and relief from suffering. In moments when mindful walking practice feels like a slog, we can turn to the teachings for support through reading books on mindful walking and mindfulness, listening to talks, or attending classes and retreats.

COMMUNITY: This is the network of practitioners of various forms of mindfulness worldwide, and we reach out to them in person or online for guidance, suggestions, and camaraderie on the path. There are more and more centers forming around the world, especially in major cities but also in rural areas, offering teachings and community in various forms.

Conclusion: Why We Walk

The American philosopher and naturalist Henry D. Thoreau wrote in his 1862 essay, "Walking," that he rarely met someone "who understood the art of Walking . . . who had a genius, so to speak, for sauntering." He traces the etymology of "sauntering" to *sans terre*, meaning without land or a home, or "having no particular home, but equally at home everywhere. For this is the secret of successful sauntering."

Being *equally at home everywhere* is the essence of mindful walking. It speaks to another of the paradoxes on this path: *doing* mindful walking, our goal is a way of *being*. We walk to cultivate mindfulness, a sense of being at ease and at home, inside ourselves, wherever we are, whatever is happening. We're at home everywhere because we carry home, a sense of well-being, within us.

This view stretches us, because it requires us to let go of the idea that peace or happiness is a thing or place only found somewhere in the world, and life is a search for it.

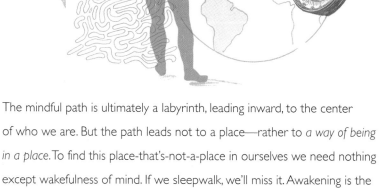

The mindful path is ultimately a labyrinth, leading inward, to the center of who we are. But the path leads not to a place—rather to *a way of being in a place*. To find this place-that's-not-a-place in ourselves we need nothing except wakefulness of mind. If we sleepwalk, we'll miss it. Awakening is the flash of insight that our true home is a way of being, in any place, and what's more, in our own mind and body.

Each time we walk mindfully, it's a dawn of something new—a new way of seeing ourselves and the world around us. Mindful awareness shines bright, not on any thing, but in a process continually unfolding, and there is always more to discover. As Thoreau wrote in the last lines of *Walden*, his masterpiece on simplicity and living each moment: "Only that day dawns to which we are awake. There is more day to dawn. The sun is but a morning star."

Conclusion: Each Walk a Pilgrimage

On the paths to Mecca and Santiago de Compostela, and around Mount Kailash in Tibet, people walk on great spiritual quests. Some devotees of Tibetan Buddhism walk several years to attend a ceremonial gathering led by the Dalai Lama. The most dedicated pause to touch their foreheads to the ground after each single step, embodying remarkable devotion.

Most of us may never have such exotic experiences of single-minded intention, but we can make any walk a pilgrimage by dedicating it to an ideal we hold dear. A pilgrimage is a journey infused with an intention that transcends mundane goals, nurturing our higher self. Such a walk can be in a new or a familiar place, and the possible intentions are limitless. It may be to connect with the healing power of nature; to care for the soul; to honor a loss or transition; to embrace mystery; to seek clarity about a decision; to affirm that we are safe in the body and

"WE SHALL NOT

CEASE FROM EXPLORATION

AND THE END OF ALL OUR EXPLORING

WILL BE TO ARRIVE WHERE WE STARTED

AND KNOW THE PLACE FOR THE

FIRST TIME."

—T.S. ELIOT

mind, no matter what we feel; to stop running from what we have been trying to avoid; to claim our power to take action on some difficult issue; or to cultivate patience, acceptance, forgiveness, or generosity.

A walk taken with intention reinforces mindfulness. Such walks are a pilgrimage in the service of insight, wisdom, and clear awareness. As you set out, pause and close your eyes, focusing your mind on the intention you wish to bring to fruition. Commit to the intention of your pilgrimage fully, letting it be strengthened and discovered anew with each touch of foot to ground.

Index

About the Author

Douglas Baker has worn out many perfectly reasonable shoes in his practice of mindful walking. He often sits down to do some seated meditation as well. He's the owner of three bicycles and countless yoga mats. When he isn't biking, walking, doing yoga, or meditating, he writes, gives talks, and leads workshops on yoga and mindful meditation. He has a counseling practice in Cambridge, Massachusetts, where he uses yoga and meditation as medicinal practices. He considers being a parent and the luxury of walking to work among life's great riches.